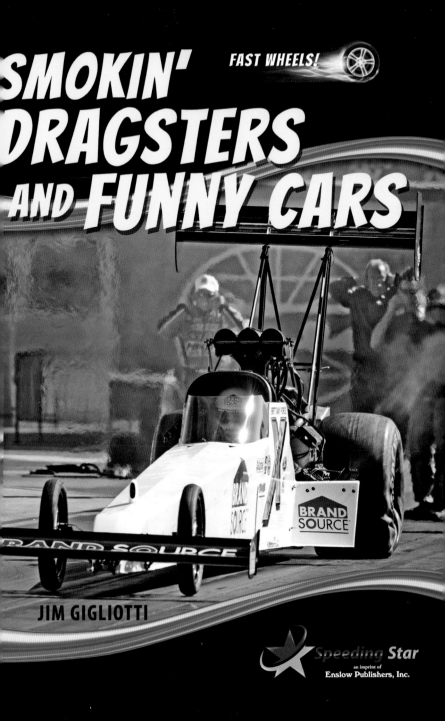

FAST WHEELS!

SMOKIN' DRAGSTERS AND FUNNY CARS

JIM GIGLIOTTI

Speeding Star
an imprint of
Enslow Publishers, Inc.

Library of Congress Cataloging-in-Publication Data

Gigliotti, Jim.
  Smokin' dragsters and funny cars / Jim Gigliotti.
      pages cm. — (Fast wheels!)
  Includes bibliographical references and index.
  Summary: "Learn about drag racing, funny cars, and experience what it feels like to spend the day at a drag race"—Provided by publisher.
  ISBN 978-1-62285-070-9
  1. Dragsters—Juvenile literature. 2. Funny cars—Juvenile literature. I. Title.
  TL236.2.G55 2013
  629.228--dc23
                                    2012047632

Future Editions
Paperback ISBN: 978-1-62285-071-6
EPUB ISBN: 978-1-62285-073-0
Single-User PDF ISBN: 978-1-62285-084-6
Multi-User PDF ISBN: 978-1-62285-159-1

Printed in the United States of America

072013 Lake Book Manufacturing, Inc., Melrose Park, IL

10 9 8 7 6 5 4 3 2 1

To Our Readers: We have done our best to make sure all Internet addresses in this book were active and appropriate when we went to press. However, the author and the Publisher have no control over, and assume no liability for, the material available on those Internet sites or on other Web sites they may link to. Any comments or suggestions can be sent by e-mail to comments@speedingstar.com or to the following address:

Speeding Star
Box 398, 40 Industrial Road
Berkeley Heights, NJ 07922
USA
www.speedingstar.com

Photo Credits: AP Images, p. 7; AP Images/Ben Margot, p. 8; AP Images/*Brainerd Dispatch*/Steve Kohls, pp. 29, 44; AP Images/Cal Sports Media, p. 1; AP Images/Cal Sports Media/Josh Homberg, p. 27; AP Images/*Indianapolis Star-The Indianapolis News*/V.A. Atkins, p. 41; AP Images/Jack Dempsey, p. 18; AP Images/NHRA, p. 31 (motorcycle); AP Images/NHRA/Bob Johnson, p. 4; AP Images/NHRA/Jerry Foss, p. 3; AP Images/NHRA/Marc Gewertz, pp. 20, 32; AP Images/NHRA/Teresa Long, pp. 15, 39; AP Images/RacersEdgePhotography/Ken Skulte, p. 36; ©Corel Corporation, pp. 17, 23, 25, 30, 31 (truck); R. Gino Santa Maria/Shutterstock.com, p. 24.

Cover Photo: AP Images/Cal Sports Media

CONTENTS

Tony Schumacher, in the U.S. Army dragster, pulls away from Brandon Bernstein during a qualifying run at the 2013 Winternationals.

WHAT IS DRAG RACING?

It is a hot day at a long, thin racetrack in Pomona, in Southern California. Two of the fastest vehicles on Earth are ready to sprint side-by-side down a quarter-mile track. They are Top Fuel dragsters competing at the famous Winternationals drag-racing event in 2006. Flames shoot out of the headers, or exhaust pipes, of one of the dragsters as they rumble at the starting line.

The engines roar. The ground shakes. The starting lights count down. As the green lights appear, so does a cloud of smoke, with an ear-splitting crack—and they're off! The two cars are a blur as they power down the track. The race is over in a few seconds, but the powerful machines reached as much as 330 miles per hour (mph)!

The fans cheer wildly. The dragster driven by fan-favorite Melanie Troxel crosses the finish line just in front of her rival, Tony Schumacher. The race is so close that only the most high-tech equipment can prove that Troxel's car has finished ahead of Schumacher's by less than a second.

It is a scene like no other in American sports. A drag-racing meet is a whirlwind of colors, sights, and sounds. It takes just a few seconds for the fastest racers to zoom down the track and cross the finish line. But drag racing is a lot more than just the five or six seconds of the race. The drivers of drag racing have a passion for racing cars.

THE HISTORY OF DRAG RACING

Experts generally agree that modern drag racing began in Southern California in the late 1940s or early 1950s. The dry bed of the Los Angeles River was one place owners raced their cars. The cars were called hot rods, and were "souped-up." That means that the cars' engines were faster and more powerful than those in regular cars. The hot rods raced side-by-side on a straight track.

Those races were illegal—not to mention dangerous. But in 1951, the National Hot Rod Association (NHRA) was formed. The NHRA began working to find places for drivers to race that were safer and legal. Soon, tracks opened in places such as Santa Ana, California, and Pomona, California. The NHRA made up rules for drag racing.

A "starter" leaps into the air waving a flag to signal the start of a drag race in Florida in 1954.

O, CHRISTMAS TREE

A pole of colorful starting lights tells the drivers when a race is about to start. This signal pole is called the "Christmas Tree" for its bright colors. The tree is located between the two racers in the center of the track.

As the drivers approach the starting line, the top row of yellow lights comes on. Then the cars inch forward to touch the line. That is when the second row of yellow lights comes on. Soon, the next three rows light up. The drivers know the race is about to start!

When the two green lights near the bottom of the tree light up, it is time to put the pedal to the metal. Jumping off the starting line at the green lights is a big part of winning a race. If the driver waits too long, his or her opponent gets a head start. But if the driver goes too soon, a red light at the bottom will signal a foul. That means the driver is disqualified and has to leave the race.

In the 1950s and 1960s television began bringing drag racing into Americans' living rooms. This helped the sport grow in popularity. By the 1970s, drag racing had a huge following. Racers such as Don Prudhomme, Don Garlits, and Shirley Muldowney became famous. Today, drivers such as Antron Brown, Tony Schumacher, John Force, Morgan Lucas, and others carry on the tradition.

TYPES OF DRAG RACING

There are three main types of drag racing: Top Fuel, Funny Car, and Pro Stock. Top Fuel dragsters are long and thin. They are the fastest of all the drag racing cars. Funny Cars and Pro Stock cars look more like regular cars.

Professional NHRA drivers compete in these categories, plus Pro Stock Motorcycle. Professionals, or "pros," are people who make money performing a certain skill—in this case, drag racing.

In addition to earning money, professional drivers earn points for where they finish at each racing event during the season. At the end of the season, the driver

WHAT'S IN A NAME?

Drag racing's stars have had some colorful nicknames. Don Garlits, one of the most famous drag racers ever, was called "Big Daddy" by an announcer at the 1962 U.S. Nationals. The nickname stuck.

Funny Car star Don Prudhomme was called "The Snake" because of his lightning-quick starts. Tom McEwen was one of Prudhomme's top rivals. He was called "The Mongoose" because that is one of the few animals that can beat a snake. Robert Hight carries a very catchy nickname: "Top Gun." He earned it by winning so often.

Lots of other stars had nicknames, too. Shirley Muldowney was called "Cha-Cha." Ed McCulloch was "Ace." And Tommy Ivo was called "T.V. Tommy" because he was one of the original Mouseketeers on the popular *Mickey Mouse Club* television show in the 1950s.

with the most points wins the championship. There is a champion for each type of drag racing.

THE BASICS

A drag race is a competition between two vehicles. The object is to see which of the two can cover a short, straight distance, starting from a standstill, in the shortest amount of time. The distance is usually a quarter of a mile. That is the same as one lap around a regulation running track, or almost four-and-a-half football fields long. The first drag racer to cross the finish line wins.

Racers compete against each other in drag meets. First, they make qualifying runs. During the qualifying runs, drivers are competing against the clock and not against each other. Qualifying runs are made to decide the 16 racers who have the lowest elapsed time. Elapsed time (ET) is the total time the run takes from start to finish.

The 16 qualifiers are then paired one-against-one in elimination races. After one round, the field is left with eight winners. After the next round, there are four drivers left. And then there are only two. Those two drivers race against each other in the finals. The winner of that race is

SAFETY FIRST—AND ALWAYS!

Operating any vehicle at high speeds is DANGEROUS. Special training and safety equipment are needed. The drivers you see at the track and on television, or that you read about, have many years of experience. They use the most modern safety equipment. Their vehicles are built and taken care of according to NHRA rules.

Even with all of these precautions, drag racing is still dangerous for experienced drivers. In 2010, two NHRA drivers were killed. Neal Parker died on June 11 when his parachutes never opened during a qualifying race for the SuperNationals. Exactly one month later on July 11, Mark Niver's car had the parachutes ripped off of his car. When he crashed, the chassis was forced into the cockpit and Niver was killed.

the champion of the drag meet. Some of the elimination races are so close that times are computed to one one-thousandth of a second!

It seems simple. The fastest car will have the lowest elapsed time and end up winning the race—right? Not necessarily. It is possible for the winner of an elimination race to have a higher ET. It depends on how the driver handles the car on the track. ET is not a factor in an elimination-round victory, but it is still an important concept for drivers. When a driver wins an elimination round with a higher ET than his or her competitor, it is called a "holeshot" victory.

TOP FUEL DRAGSTERS

Top Fuel cars are the fastest of all the drag racing cars. They can reach speeds of more than 300 mph. It can take them as little as four-and-a-half seconds to cover a quarter-mile drag race track. Do not blink—or you might miss the race!

These dragsters are instantly recognizable by their long, thin frames. How long are they? A Top Fuel dragster's wheelbase is 285 to 300 inches—that is up to 25 feet long! Compare that with the wheelbase of a typical passenger car, which is around 110 inches— just over nine feet. (Wheelbase is the distance between the center of the front wheel and the center of the rear

As a Top Fuel dragster sprints off the starting line, its engine generates so much power that it creates a fireball!

wheel.) Top Fuel dragsters are only a few feet high except for a tall wing on the back. The wing is designed to direct air currents for faster performance.

A Top Fuel dragster's engine is at the back of the vehicle for the driver's safety. This way, if something goes wrong with the engine, the problem stays behind the driver.

Every Top Fuel dragster has a small wheelie bar on its back end. A "wheelie" is when the front end of a car lifts off the ground and the car balances on its back wheels. Top Fuel dragsters go at such high speeds and are so heavy in the back that they can easily wheelie, and possibly flip over. The wheelie bar keeps the front end from lifting too far off the ground.

These amazing vehicles do not run on regular gasoline. Instead, they run on a fuel called nitromethane, sometimes called "nitro." It is much more powerful than regular gasoline. In fact, nitromethane has even been used for rocket fuel.

Top Fuel dragsters are so powerful that they can accelerate, or increase their speed, faster than a fighter jet. Some Top Fuel dragsters can have more than 6,000 horsepower (hp) in their engines. Horsepower is a

This simply colored Top Fuel dragster was one of the earlier long-bodied cars.

WHERE THE RUBBER MEETS THE ROAD

The tires on a Top Fuel dragster are called "slicks." That is because they do not have any treads. The treads on a regular car's tires are the grooves that help them better grip the road. But for a Top Fuel dragster, "no grooves" means that more of the tire hits the road. And that means the tire can pull the dragster along faster.

The back tires of a Top Fuel dragster are about 18 inches wide and about 118 inches around. The front tires are much smaller, closer to the size of airplane or bike tires.

Top Fuel drag racing is tough on tires! The cars' high speeds create high temperatures, which wear the tires out quickly. The large back tires usually last only about four to six drag racing runs. Compare that with the life of regular car tires. Most of those can last as many as 40,000 to 50,000 miles. Four to six runs for a dragster is only one to one and a half miles!

measure of engine performance. It compares the power created by one horse to what an engine can do. This means it would take 6,000 horses working together to produce enough power to drive a Top Fuel dragster at top speed! A regular passenger car has around 150 hp. A Top Fuel dragster has more than forty times more power!

Top Fuel dragsters beat the world's fastest sports cars, too. For example, the Porsche Carrera GT can accelerate from zero to 60 mph in about 3.8 seconds. But the fastest Top Fuel cars can reach 100 mph in only eight-tenths of a second!

THE WORLD'S FASTEST

The current record holder for speed in a Top Fuel dragster is Tony Schumacher. In 2005 he reached a top speed of 337.58 mph during a race in Brainerd, Minnesota.

According to the NHRA, the quickest that a Top Fuel dragster has covered a quarter mile is 3.701 seconds. Antron Brown set that elapsed time world record on October 8, 2012. He did it while competing against Brandon Bernstein in the semifinals of an event at Mohnton, Pennsylvania.

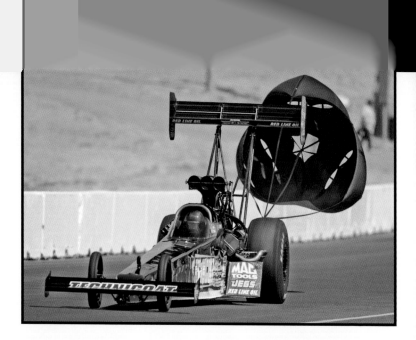

HANGING OUT THE LAUNDRY

Speeds of more than 300 mph are too fast for brakes alone to slow down a dragster on a quarter-mile track. So when a driver crosses the finish line, he or she pulls a lever inside the car to release a parachute from the back of the car. This is known as "hanging out the laundry."

The parachute acts as a powerful "brake." When the car has slowed down enough, the driver can then stop it using the regular brakes. If a driver releases the parachute late, or the parachute does not work properly, the car slides into a giant sandpit at the end of the drag strip. The sand helps to stop the car safely.

Many feel that Schumacher is the best Top Fuel driver ever. In 2009, he won Top Fuel's overall season points championship for the sixth year in a row and for the seventh time in his career. That is more than any other driver.

FUNNY CARS

Funny Cars got their name because they look like regular cars—sort of. But when you look closer, they seem a little "funny." First of all, there are no doors. And there is no passenger seat or back seat. Also, the entire body of the car lifts up so mechanics can work on the engine. In fact, a Funny Car driver gets in and out of the car when the body is lifted up.

If there is an emergency during a race, though, he or she can open up an escape hatch (door) in the roof. Like Top Fuel dragsters, Funny Cars run on a fuel mixture made up mostly of nitromethane. Unlike a Top Fuel dragster, though, a Funny Car's engine is at the front of the car.

From far away, Funny Cars appear to look like regular passenger cars. But Funny Cars are actually very different. For one thing, they don't have doors.

Funny Cars cannot reach speeds as fast as Top Fuel dragsters, but they are not too far behind. Ron Capps holds the record for the fastest run in a Funny Car. He needed only 3.964 seconds to go from start to finish in a qualifying session in Englishtown, New Jersey, in 2012. That is just a quarter of a second slower than Antron Brown's Top Fuel record. The record for the top speed

ANATOMY OF A FUNNY CAR

The NHRA has certain rules about features that all Funny Cars must have. Here are some of those features:

• A Funny Car must weigh at least 2,300 POUNDS. Also, the front part of it must be at least three inches off the ground and the rest must be at least two inches off the ground.

• The ENGINE must be built and adjusted according to very technical NHRA rules. It takes an expert mechanic to follow them!

• All drivers must be buckled into a SAFETY RESTRAINT (seat belt) system. They also must wear fireproof suits. All cars must carry a fire extinguisher. The underside of the car's body needs to have a special coating that will not burn.

• The outside SHELL must be made of graphite and weigh between 87 and 89 pounds. Much of the outer shell is just for show. It does not offer the protection that the outside of a regular car does.

• The large REAR SPOILER on the back of a Funny Car must be mounted on, not built in (as some are on regular cars). The rear spoiler forces air down on the rear tires and makes the car go faster.

• The back tires must be SLICKS that are 18 inches wide and 118 inches around. The front tires on a Funny Car are much smaller.

• The WHEELBASE must be between 100 and 125 inches. The wheelbase is measured from the middle of the front wheel to the middle of the back wheel.

in a Funny Car is Mike Ashley's mark of 334.32 mph. It is only about 3 mph slower than Schumacher's Top Fuel record.

Some of the most popular drivers in the history of car racing have been Funny Car drivers. John Force is one of them. Starting in the late 1980s, he became one of the greatest Funny Car drivers ever. He is still one of the best today! Force has won more national drag racing events than anyone else in history. In 1996, he became the first drag racing driver to be named the National Motorsports

Jerry Caminito blasts down the road in his "Blue Thunder" Funny car. Caminito is known for walking away from the worst accident in NHRA history.

Driver of the Year. That honor usually goes to a NASCAR driver or an Indy car driver. From 1993 to 2002, Force won ten-straight season points championships in the Funny Car class.

Force turned sixty-three during the 2012 season, but he was still in the Top 10 of the points standings. In fact, he is so popular that he and his three Funny Car-racing daughters starred in a reality television show called *Driving Force*. His daughter Ashley started entering NHRA Funny Car events in 2007. She was a top driver until her retirement in 2012. Force's other daughters, Courtney and Brittany, are also drag-racing stars.

WOMEN RACERS

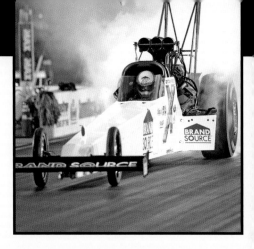

In drag racing, women compete equally with men. That was not always the case. It was Shirley Muldowney who helped pave the way for today's women racers. Muldowney is a member of the Motorsports Hall of Fame. She was not the first woman driver in drag racing, but she is the most famous. Many people who do not even follow racing know her name.

"Cha-Cha," as Muldowney was called, made her mark in Funny Cars beginning in 1971. That year, she won her first major meet in a Funny Car. She moved to Top Fuel in 1974 and went on to win three NHRA season championships. She did it even though she faced many male drivers who did not think that a woman should be competing with men.

Today, women are major competitors in all classes of drag racing. In fact, drivers such as Leah Pruett and Brittany Force often qualify for the final 16 at Top Fuel drag meets. Courtney Force and Alexis DeJoria are two of the top Funny Car drivers. Erica Enders-Stevens is a popular Pro Stock driver who already has a handful of wins to her credit.

PRO STOCK RACING

Many people would like it if their cars could go as fast as a dragster. But that would be dangerous—and against the law! Besides, regular cars are not built to race at the speeds of a dragster. A regular car could never handle that type of intense driving.

But if you go to an NHRA drag race or watch one on television, you might notice that some of the cars look a little like the cars you see on the street. Are those regular cars? No—those are Pro Stock cars. Of all the drag racing cars, Pro Stock cars look the most like regular cars. The term "stock" means that they are a regular automobile style. But of course that regular style has been modified, or changed, for racing.

Erica Enders-Stevens in the black car has just beaten her opponent, Allen Johnson. This gave Enders-Stevens one of the top qualifying times of the day at the 2012 Lucas Oil NHRA Nationals.

For example, a Pro Stock car has a much more powerful engine than a regular car. These engines are also extremely expensive to build. In fact, the NHRA says that most Pro Stock engines cost more than $80,000 to build. That is a lot more than an entire passenger car costs, even with all the extras!

Another way that Pro Stock and regular cars differ is that most of a Pro Stock car's body is made of fiberglass, which is lighter than steel. Most of a regular car's body is made of steel.

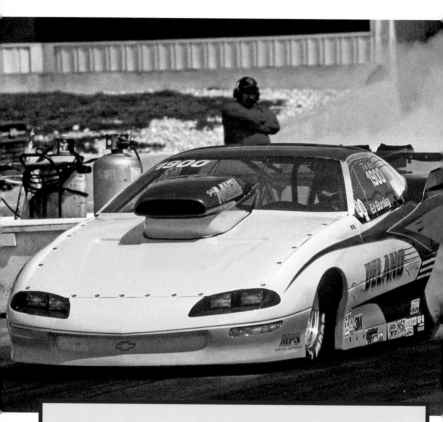

Of all the drag racing cars, Pro Stock vehicles look the most like regular cars. This one is a modified mid 1990s Chevy Camaro, run by Ed Burnley.

THEY RACE THOSE?

Top Fuel, Funny Car, and Pro Stock are the most well-known types of drag racing. But they are just three of more than 200 types of NHRA drag racing. Many do not even use cars. In fact, two more of the most popular types of drag racing use trucks and motorcycles.

MONSTER TRUCK DRAG RACING

Imagine huge pickup trucks racing each other on a dirt track at 50 or 55 mph and crushing cars parked in their way. Yes, there are even drag racing competitions for Monster Trucks! Like at other drag-racing events, Monster Trucks race one-against-one. But these huge vehicles race on shorter tracks that are littered with obstacles, including cars, to run over and crush.

MOTORCYCLE DRAG RACING

Pro Stock motorcycles cover the quarter-mile track almost as fast as Pro Stock cars do. The fastest motorcycles go almost 200 mph. They usually cross the finish line in about seven seconds. The record is 6.728 seconds, set by Andrew Hines in Mohnton, Pennsylvania, in 2012. Edward Krawiec set the top speed record of 199.26 mph at Gainesville, Florida, in 2011.

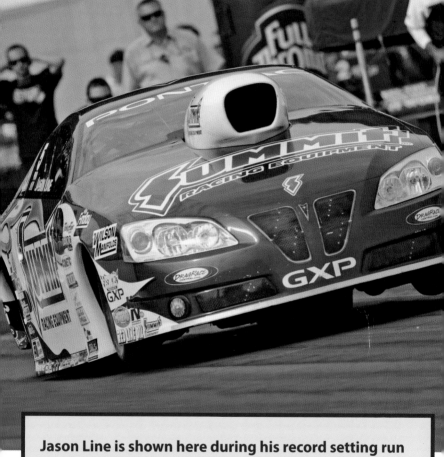

Jason Line is shown here during his record setting run for the fastest time record set on October 3, 2011.

Pro Stock cars are also different from other drag racing cars. For example, a Pro Stock car has a wheelbase of 99 to 105 inches. That is much shorter than a Top Fuel dragster. And unlike Top Fuel and Funny Cars, Pro Stock cars run on gasoline. But this is not ordinary gasoline— it is high-octane gasoline. All gasoline is given a number called an octane rating, which measures certain features of the gasoline. The higher the octane rating is, the better the car's engine performance will be.

There are strict rules for everything about a Pro Stock car. That includes its engine, its brakes, and its weight. As in all classes of drag racing, NHRA officials inspect Pro Stock vehicles before and after every event. They need to make sure every driver is competing fairly.

THE BEST IN PRO STOCK

On October 3, 2011, Jason Line made the fastest run ever in a Pro Stock car. He raced the quarter mile in 6.477 seconds in his Pontiac GTO in Mohnton, Pennsylvania. On October 8, 2012, he set a new speed record of 214.35 mph. In 2006, Line originally broke the record held by Greg Anderson. Anderson is one of the top Pro Stock racers around today. He won the overall points championship three seasons in a row, from 2003 to 2005. He won again in 2010 and finished in the Top 3 each year from 2002 to 2011.

One of the best Pro Stock drivers of all time was Bob Glidden. He won the season points title an amazing ten times. From 1985 to 1989, he won the championship every year. Glidden usually was so much faster than everyone else that he had the fastest qualifying run in an amazing 23 races in a row during the late 1980s!

5

RACE WEEKEND

The green light flashed, and Robert Hight was off in an instant. His Ford Mustang roared down the track at near-record speed. And yet, he could not seem to pull away from rival Whit Bazemore in the Funny Car final of the 2006 U.S. Nationals. "We went 328 miles per hour and it seemed like it took forever to get to the finish line," he said. But suddenly, it was over. "Forever" took 4.737 seconds, and Hight crossed the finish line less than two-hundredths of a second faster than Bazemore. Hight was the U.S. Nationals champion!

Becoming the U.S. Nationals champion is a drag race driver's ultimate dream because it is drag racing's most important event. Football has the Super Bowl.

Robert Hight celebrates after winning the 2006 Mac Tools U.S. Nationals.

NASCAR has the Daytona 500. And drag racing has the U.S. Nationals, nicknamed "The Big Go."

Drag racing fans from all over the country gather in Clermont, Indiana, on Labor Day weekend each year for four days of exciting racing at the U.S. Nationals. Clermont is just outside of Indianapolis, which is the most famous racing town in America. Men and women, old and young, travel to "Indy" for the U.S. Nationals.

In 2011, more than 80 competitors entered the Big Go in the three main race classifications: Top Fuel, Funny Car, and Pro Stock. After three days of qualifying, the field was narrowed down to the 48 fastest competitors (16 in each class).

Each year, the Nationals begin with qualifying runs in each class on Friday. This is a good time to get up close to the competitors and watch the crews in action. That is because they are not yet feeling the intense pressure of the final day of racing. They are more likely to spend time with the fans and answer their questions. Plus, this early in the competition, the crowds are not quite as big.

Before each run, the drivers do their burnouts. That means they spin their tires in a shallow puddle of water located close to the starting line. Spinning the tires heats them and cleans them for better traction on the racetrack. It also sends smoke into the air and gets the crowd going. The fans know a race is about to begin!

After each qualifying run, mechanics, also known as "wrenches," work like crazy in the garage. They are fixing leaks, checking fuel systems, servicing the engine— whatever needs to be done. Everything must be perfect for the next time the driver gets on the track.

QUALIFYING

Most events have two days of qualifying runs. But the U.S. Nationals is such a big event that there are three days of qualifying. By Labor Day on Monday, each class has been cut down to the 16 drivers with the fastest times. They race against each other in the first round of elimination races. The driver with the fastest qualifying time races against the driver with the slowest qualifying time. The second fastest driver races against the second slowest, and so on.

In the Funny Car class at the 2011 U.S. Nationals, Mike Neff qualified ninth. His time of 4.747 seconds in his first qualifying run made him look as if he had the least powerful Funny Car in the meet. In his first-round

Mike Neff doesn't have to worry about his speed after earning the No. 1 qualifying time at the 2012 Gatornationals in Gainesville, Florida.

elimination race against Robert Hight, Neff got off to a poor start, yet still managed to pull out a victory. Luckily for Neff, Hight's car lost a cylinder and he was out of the competition. Neff went on to win the meet. Hight received nothing but heartbreak. There are no do-overs in drag racing. It is "one and done." One mistake or problem and a driver is out of the competition. That is something else that makes drag racing such a thrilling sport.

Jim Head found that out the hard way in 2006. He crossed the finish line first in a close race against Whit Bazemore. But Head was disqualified after his car touched one of the blocks in the center of the track. If any part of the car hits the blocks, it means it has gone into the middle of the track. And if a driver crosses into the middle of the track, he or she is disqualified.

SAFETY

It was Friday, February 13, 2012, during a qualifying round for the Pro Stock races at zMAX Dragway in Concord, North Carolina. Matt Hagan had a terrifying explosion. His car made it about halfway down the track

Safety is of the utmost importance while racing, or doing any type of driving. Drivers risk their lives every time they step onto the track and some don't make it home.

before the car just exploded, sending the car into hundreds of pieces.

Emergency crews were on the scene right away. The fire was put out, and Hagan was checked for injuries. He was lucky to walk away from the wreck with no injuries, let alone alive. Hagan's safety equipment did its job.

Safety is the biggest concern for the NHRA and its drivers and crews. If an accident happens, emergency workers are right on the spot. And a helicopter can quickly bring an injured driver to the nearest hospital if necessary. Just a few seconds' difference might save a life.

THE WINNERS

Sometimes a driver knows his opponent has a more powerful or better-running car. In that case, the driver's best chance is to beat the other racer off the starting line. In fact, that is one of the few strategies drag racing drivers need to use to win a race.

For example, in the Pro Stock final at the 2006 U.S. Nationals, Dave Connolly knew that Greg Anderson had been running better times throughout the weekend. So he tried to take off faster at the green light. But he jumped too soon. Connolly got a red light and was disqualified. Anderson won the race, as well as the championship.

In Top Fuel, Tony Schumacher won his fifth U.S. Nationals Championship by beating Brandon Bernstein in the final. And in the Funny Car class, Robert Hight beat Whit Bazemore in that super-tight finish. As it is every year, the 2006 "Big Go" was a thrill for both drivers and fans.

Drag racing is a simple sport. Racers need to be the first off the starting line to shoot straight down a quarter-mile track and be the first to cross the finish line. But simple does not mean easy. These drivers have years of

WHERE CAN I WATCH?

The annual NHRA Mello Yello tour visits twenty cities in many parts of the United States. The 2013 season started in February with the Winternationals in Pomona, California. One month later, the drag racers stopped nearly 2,500 miles away, in Gainesville, Florida.

If you are not anywhere near a Mello Yello event on the NHRA main circuit, there are still plenty of local races to find. Check out NHRA.com for a list of tracks all over the United States. The Web site also lists the meets, special events, and regular shows on television each week. Even if you cannot make it to the track, you can still catch much of the excitement on TV.

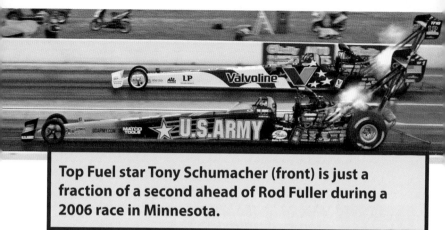

Top Fuel star Tony Schumacher (front) is just a fraction of a second ahead of Rod Fuller during a 2006 race in Minnesota.

experience and know how to handle their powerful Top Fuel, Funny Car, and Pro Stock drag racing cars. They face danger in each race. And as in every sport, drag racing has many rules. But the strategy is simple: drive the fastest and win!

BURNOUT—When a driver spins the wheels of his or her car in water to heat and clean them so they will better grip the track.

CHRISTMAS TREE—Electronic starting lights between the lanes of a drag racing track that signal the start of a race.

DISQUALIFIED—No longer allowed to compete in the current race.

ELAPSED TIME (ET)—The time measured from the moment a dragster begins moving off the starting line until it crosses the finish line.

ELIMINATION RACE—Race at a drag meet in which the winner advances to the next round.

GRAPHITE—Soft, black mineral that is flexible but very strong. It is used to make the bodies of race cars. Its light weight will not slow down a dragster.

HATCH—Opening in the roof of a Funny Car through which a driver can escape in case of emergency.

HEADERS—Exhaust pipes that carry burned gas out of the engine.

NITROMETHANE—Also called "nitro." Powerful fuel used in Top Fuel dragsters.

OCTANE—A number rating assigned to measure certain features of gasoline. The higher the number, the better the engine performance.

QUALIFYING RUN—A timed individual run on a drag-racing track, taken by each driver. The 16 drivers with the best qualifying runs get to compete in the elimination races.

SPOILER—A device on the back of a Funny Car or Pro Stock car that directs air currents to improve the car's speed.

WHEELIE BAR—Bar on the back end of a dragster that keeps the front wheels from lifting too far off the ground.

WRENCH—Nickname for a mechanic who works on a drag racing team.

FIND OUT MORE

BOOKS

Georgiou, Tyrone. *Pro Stock Dragsters*. New York, N.Y.: Gareth Stevens, 2011.

Kelley, K.C. *Drag Racing*. Tarrytown, N.Y.: Marshall Cavendish Benchmark, 2010.

McKenna, Kevin. *How to Drag Race*. North Branch, MN.: CarTech, 2008.

Miller, Timothy. *Drag Racing: The World's Fastest Sport*. Richmond Hill, ON.: Firefly Books, 2012.

INTERNET ADDRESSES

HTTP://WWW.DRAGLIST.COM

This Web site pulls together pictures, statistics, and stories from every form of drag racing.

HTTP://WWW.JOHNFORCE.COM

The official Web site of John Force Racing, one of drag racing's most popular and successful teams.

HTTP://WWW.NHRA.COM

The National Hot Rod Association's schedules, results, and driver profiles, plus a detailed history section.

.